Smile Please!

by
Shelagh McGee

Prentice-Hall, Inc., Englewood Cliffs, New Jersey

First American edition published 1978 by
Prentice-Hall, Inc.

Printed in Great Britain by BAS Printers Limited,
Over Wallop, Hampshire

Library of Congress Cataloging in Publication Data

McGee, Shelagh.
    Smile please.

    SUMMARY: Auntie Ruth, Cousin Bert, and other family
members are described in poetry.
    1. Family—juvenile poetry. 2. Humorous
    poetry, English. [1. Family—poetry. 2. Humorous
    poetry. 3. English poetry.] I. Title.
PZ8.3.M1565Sm   1978   821'.9'14   77-27880
ISBN 0-13-814558-X

To all my family

Smile Please!

There's Uncle Joe and Auntie Flo
Standing at the back,
And next to them there's Cousin Em
With her brand-new husband Jack;
In front of these stands Uncle Keith
With daughters Mag and Pat,
And Great-Aunt Cora and her lodger Dora,
Who always wears a hat.
The next one down, (the one with the frown)
Is Cousin Jane's fiance,
He wears silk ties
I think he tries
To look too smart and fancy.
Then next to him is Uncle Jim,
An athlete large and strong,
Who smiles all day at Auntie May—
They've not been married long.
To the right of her is Cousin Clare
Who dresses like a hippie,
All dangling beads and hair like weeds—
I frankly think she's drippy.
The next two men are Frank and Len,
My cousin and my brother,
And then there's Dad, who's looking sad,
Then me, our cat, and Mother.

My Mother

My Mother's soft and sort of round,
She has bright yellow hair,
Her favorite dress is pink and green,
She wears it everywhere;
Her mouth is red, she laughs a lot,
Her teeth are square and white,
She wears shoes with tall thin heels
When she goes out at night.
She's good at knitting jumpers
And baking birthday cakes,
And beating Dad at poker—
They play for quite high stakes.

Dad

I like my Dad;
His hair is red,
His nose is long,
His arms are strong.
I like my Dad;
His feet are big,
His hands are square,
He doesn't care.
I like my Dad;
He plays a lot,
I like his smile,
My Dad's got style.

Baby....

I'm the baby small and pink,
I smell of soap and milk,
I have to wear a frilly dress,
With ribbons of blue silk;
But I'm allowed to make a noise,
To yell and scream and shout,
And suck my thumb and dribble,
And throw my food about.

... *Brother*

And I am his big brother,
He's one and I'm eleven,
And when he's put to bed at six,
I'm in my seventh heaven.

My Sister's Knitting

My sister's sitting knitting,
Each day she'll sit and knit,
Clicking garments into shape,
Wondering who they'll fit.
Long johns for Uncle Arthur,
Who tends to feel the cold,
(It's one of the discomforts
Of being rather old).
Short socks for Cousin Doris,
Who does a lot of walking;
A muffler for Gladys
Who does a lot of talking.
For Grandmama a bonnet,
(Two plain, three purl, slip one),
And this round thing's a cushion
For the cat to sit upon.
My sister's sitting knitting,
And I am all agog
To see my sister fitting
Woolly bloomers on the dog!

Taking a Rain-check

Rain stopped play
In the garden today,
I'd have stayed there all day,
If I could;
My mother insisted,
Although I resisted,
By dragging my feet in the mud.
I was dragged up the path,
Then dumped in the bath,
And made horribly, thoroughly clean—
It's days like today,
that drive me to say,
That mothers can be very mean!!

A Dogged Tale

For my dog I made a coat
Of handsome houndstooth tweed,
In black and white to match just right
His collar and his lead.
He tried it on—I must admit
It did look very good,
Until he sneaked out in the rain
And came back full of mud!

Bertie...

I've got an Uncle Stevie,
And I've got an Auntie Annie,
I've met my Great-Aunt Enid,
Who's sister to my Granny.
I have an Uncle Walter,
Who lives far overseas,
And I've got an Aunt Lucinda
And a cousin called Louise.
I've sisters Belle and Gertie,
And brothers Len and Tom,
And we have a cat called Bertie,
His last name's Burlington.
Poor Bertie is an orphan,
Poor cat, he's quite alone,
And he's jealous of our family
Since he has none of his own.
He frightened Great-Aunt Enid,
He punched her on the chin,
Then he sat before his victim
With an enigmatic grin.

And when our Uncle Walter,
(The one from overseas)
Came visiting one Christmas,
Our Bertie bit his knees.
He nipped our Uncle Stevie,
And hissed at poor old Granny,
Then he hid behind the TV,
And spat at Auntie Annie;
And when she dared to pull his tail,
Lucinda played with fire,
Bertie gave her a chilling stare
And scratches to admire.
But Bertie isn't always bad,
He can be very sweet—
Like in the winter, when I'm cold,
He comes to warm my feet;
He stays with me when I'm alone,
As good as good can be,
He loves me and I love him,
You see—two's company!

Grandma

Grandma's kind and sixty-three
And always busy as a bee;
She likes to jog,
She walks her dog,
She's fond of cats,
And scared of rats,
She likes to cook,
And read a book,
I'm only eight,
I think she's great.

Grandpa

Grandpa's tall and sixty-four
Or sixty-five, or maybe more;
He's been to France
And he can dance,
He's seen a king
And learned to sing;
He doesn't like fish,
But never says why,
And his favorite dish
Is shoo-fly pie.

Auntie Ruth

My Auntie Ruth
To tell the truth
Is really rather funny,
She washes her hair
With the greatest of care,
And makes shampoo with honey.
She paints her lips
And swings her hips—
My mother says she's naughty.
She wears tight skirts
And always flirts—
She says it's being sporty.

Cousin Bert

Cousin Bert
Has a very nice shirt
With Christmas trees
And mountains;
It's striped and checked
And all bedecked
With polka-dots
And fountains.
He has some pants
Which, quite by chance,
Match the dots
And the stripes to a T;
And he feels very neat
In spite of the heat,
When he walks with bare feet
By the sea.

My Aunt Grace

My Aunt Grace
Has a round brown face,
She's fond of the sea and the sun;
She has light brown hair
That's rather spare
Drawn tightly up in a bun.
She wears brown shoes
The color of stews,
In shining, strong brown leather;
She wears brown socks
And brown crepe frocks—
She wears brown, whatever the weather;
You'd think all that brown
Would be getting her down—
She is, after all, sixty-four—
But she says, "Well, my dear,
To me it seems clear,
That blue is a terrible bore,
In yellow or green
I'd be a has-been,
And I'm certain I wouldn't like red:
In plain black and white
I'm an absolute fright,
And in mauve I'd not be seen dead.
But I do feel a dream
In coffee and cream,
And chocolate goes straight to my head."

A Great Uncle

Does 'Great' in front of 'Uncle'
Mean that my Uncle's smart?
Can it mean he's excellent
At math or French or art?
Perhaps it means some honor,
A gold star from a queen,
A title, badge or medal
For the useful man he's been?
Could it be he's very tall
And overlooks the garden wall?
Could it mean he's highly-skilled,
(Like Alexander, iron-willed)?
Statesman, genius, raconteur—
To none of these does 'Great' refer—
A name as good as any other,
It simply means he's Grandma's brother.

Auntie Lizzie

Auntie Lizzie, who was so thin,
Longed for a curvy figure.
She yearned to be stout,
To be blossoming out,
To be rounded and generally bigger.
Auntie Lizzie, who was so thin,
Ate for all she was worth,
So the pounds would be added,
She'd be rounded and padded,
And put half a yard on her girth.
Auntie Lizzie, who was so thin,
Put on more and more pounds and still more,
And became so inflated—
A state she just hated—
That she slimmed, to be trim like before!

Uncle Tim

Uncle Tim was not so slim,
He'd hopes of being thinner.
He tried just having carrot juice
And lettuce leaves for dinner;
But fruit and greens and salads
Brought on uncertain moods,
He felt just like a rabbit,
Eating diet foods.
Lean meat made him feel morbid,
And few things were more depressing,
Than cottage cheese and cabbage,
Disguised in yoghurt dressing.
Now, he's taken with the theory
That we are what we eat—
And Uncle Tim's decided
That he's peachy, plump and sweet.

Romance

Old Ma Smith's son Henry
Married Auntie Jane,
He met her in the store
At the end of Lizard Lane;
He saw her weighing candy
And thought she'd do just fine,
So he bought a pound of chocolates,
And said, "Will you be mine?
You are the apple of my eye,
My sweet, my treat, my cherry pie".
They married two weeks later,
The bridesmaid was our Fanny,
Now they've got a son and daughter,
And old Ma Smith's a granny.

Cousin Horace

Cousin Horace is very bright,
His head's just packed with brain,
And though he's almost always right,
He's not what you'd call vain.
He can add up columns of figures so long—
All in his head, in a twinkling—
That you and I would be sure to get wrong,
We really would have no inkling.
Whatever subject you care to name,
No matter how horrendous,
To Horace they are all a game,
His knowledge is stupendous.
His insight into history
To me is just a mystery;
He can reel off every date,
Every battle, death and fate.
Technology, too, he knows through and through,
And he likes to converse on—And even make verse on—
His philosophical view—phew!
Every bone in the body he knows,
From the ears to the tips of the toes,
The tibia, fibula, shape of the femur,
The cause of a tumor—
There's even a rumor, I'm told,
He's discovered a cure for the cold!
Math, trigonometry, spelling,
Latin, geography, telling,
Chemistry, physics and English lit.—
At none of these is he a nit.
From all of this you'll form the view
There's simply nothing our Horace can't do;
But it's really no wonder his I.Q. is high—
His favorite dish is mathematical pie!

When I'm an aunt I shan't
Sip tea and criticize,
Won't buy my nieces socks,
Or my nephews ties.
For birthdays I'll send monkeys,
White mice and pirate suits;
At Christmas sets for chemistry,
And tambourines and flutes.
At Easter I'll bring chocolate eggs,
Not hymn books of white leather,
And I'll never scold at muddy feet
Or dogs in rainy weather.
When I'm an aunt I'll never mind
Rough ball games on my lawn,
And even turn an eye that's blind
To pillow fights at dawn.

Goodbye for Now!

A family like mine
Has quite a history,
We've pirates, farmers, cowboys,
On our crazy family tree;
Dear Aunt Grace had a Grandpa
Who used to be a clown,
And probably that's why
I've never seen her frown!
Cousin Bert's Great-Uncle
Was once a high-class tailor,
And Grandma's brother Henry
Was all his life a sailor.
Aunt Ruth's Mom was a dancer
Who used to do high kicks;
And Uncle Tim's Dad's brother
Could do great party tricks.
But there's no time like the present,
And my family of today
Are clever, kind and zany
And fun in every way;
We play games and we giggle,
We're always trouble-free,
So now, goodbye, from all of us—
When can you come to tea?